# ANCIENT ROME

## Philip Steele

KINGFISHER

**KINGFISHER**

First published 2009 by Kingfisher
an imprint of Macmillan Children's Books
a division of Macmillan Publishers Limited
The Macmillan Building, 4 Crinan Street, London N1 9XW
Basingstoke and Oxford
Associated companies throughout the world
www.panmacmillan.com

Consultant: Dr Hugh Bowden, Kings College London

Illustration by Steve Stone (represented by Artist Partners Ltd)
with additional artwork by Thomas Bayley and Kevin Jones Associates

ISBN 978-0-7534-1741-6

Copyright © Macmillan Children's Books 2009

1 3 5 7 9 8 6 4 2
1TR/02/09/SHENS/SC/126.6MA/C

A CIP catalogue record for this book is available from the British Library.

Printed in Taiwan

**Note to readers:** The website addresses listed in this book are correct at the time of publishing.
However, due to the ever-changing nature of the internet, website addresses and content can change.
Websites can contain links that are unsuitable for children. The publisher cannot be held responsible for
changes in website addresses or content, or for information obtained through third-party websites.
We strongly advise that internet searches should be supervised by an adult.

**The Publisher would like to thank the following for permission to reproduce their images (t = top, b = bottom, c = centre, r = right, l = left):**

Pages 4-5t Photolibrary/Julio Lopez Saguar; 4bl Alamy/Firstshot; 5bl Photolibrary/Nigel Blythe; 6t Shutterstock; 6-7 Photolibrary/L. Romano/Dea; 6bl Art Archive (AA)/Museo de Villa Giulia, Rome/Dagli Orti; 7cl AA/Bibliotheque des Arts Decoratifs, Paris/Dagli Orti; 7bl PA/AP/Italian Culture Ministry; 7br Digital Vision; 8 Alamy/Gari Wyn Williams; 9 Frank Lane Picture Agency/ Sarah Rowland/Holt; 10ctr AA/Dagli Orti; 10c AA/Dagli Orti; 10bl Bridgeman Art Library (BAL)/Fitzwilliam Museum University of Cambridge; 10cbl AA/Musee du Louvre/Dagli Orti; 10cbr BAL/ Musee du Louvre; 10br Alamy/London Art Archive; 12 British Museum; 13 Axiom/Chris Caldicott; 15tl Getty Images/AFP; 15br British Museum; 16-17 AA/Museo della Civita Romana/Dagli Orti; 16bl Shutterstock; 17tc Alamy/Mark Boulton; 17r Shutterstock; 18-19 Corbis/Rudy Sulgan; 18cr Alamy/David Forster; 18c Corbis/Ed Kashi; 18bc AA/Archaeology Museum, Naples/Dagli Orti; 18br AA/Museo Civico Udine/Dagli Orti; 19tl Corbis/William Manning; 19c Alamy/Gavin Heller; 19bl Corbis/Wolfgang Meier/zefa; 19br (both) AA/Dagli Orti; 20br Shutterstock; 21tr Alamy/Marco Scataglini; 23tr AA/National Museum Bucharest/Dagli Orti; 24tl Shutterstock; 24bl Shutterstock; 24c Alamy/Roger Coulam; 24cl Shutterstock; 24br Alamy/Picture Contact; 25cl Alamy/John Martin; 25c Ermine Street Guard; 25cr Alamy/Graeme Peacock; 25bl British Museum; 25br Ermine Street Guard; 27tl Alamy/Peter Horree; 27br AA/Archaeological Museum Cherchel, Algeria; 28tr Getty Images/Imagebank; 28cl British Museum; 30 Shutterstock; 32-33background Shutterstock; 32tl AA/Museo Capitolino/Dagli Orti; 32cl AA/Archaeological Museum, Naples/Dagli Orti; 32r AA/Archaeological Museum, Naples/Dagli Orti; 32c Alamy/London Art Archive; 32bc AA/Archaeological Museum, Naples/Dagli Orti; 33cl AA/Archaeology Museum, Naples/Dagli Orti; 33b BAL/Museum of London; 33tr The Ronald Grant Archive/HD Vision Studios/BBC/HBO; 34bl AA/Museo Capitolino/Dagli Orti; 35bl Corbis/Tobias Schwarz/Reuters; 37 (in order) AA/Museo Capitolino/Dagli Orti; Alamy/London Art Archive; Corbis/Araldo de Luca; Werner Forman Archive/British Museum; AA/Museo Capitolino/Dagli Orti; Corbis/Araldo de Luca; 38-39 temple background Shutterstock; 38bl AA/Archaeological Museum, Naples/Dagli Orti; 38bc AA/Musee du Louvre/Dagli Orti; 38r Getty Images/ PhotoAlto Agency; 39tl Alamy/Peter Horree; 39tr British Museum; 39bl Alamy/Richard Osbourne/Blue Pearl Photographic; 39br AA/Archaeological Museum Venice/Dagli Orti; 40-41 Corbis/Ted Spiegel; 40c Shutterstock; 40br Alamy/Martin Beddall; 41tl AA/Museo Nazionale Palazzo Altemps Rome/Dagli Orti; 41cr British Museum; 41b AA/San Vitale, Ravenna/Dagli Orti; 42-43background Shutterstock; 42bl AA/Navy Historical Service, Vincennes/Dagli Orti; 42r AA/British Library; 43cl Corbis/Vincent Kessler/Reuters; 43c Corbis/George D. Lepp; 43cl AA/Musee du Chateau de Versailles/Dagli Orti; 43bl Corbis/Bob Krist; 43br PA/AP/Marianna Bertagnolli; 46-47 AA/Museo della Civita Romana/Dagli Orti; 47r Rex Features; 48l Shutterstock/Vera Bogaerts; 48cl Art Archive/Villa of the Mysteries Pompeii/Dagli Orti; 48bl Shutterstock/Pavle Marjanovic; 48tr Photolibrary/Davis McCardle; 48br The Little Entertainment Group

# CONTENTS

CIVILIZATION – *a society that has developed laws, government, arts, sciences and technology*

"CIVIS ROMANUS SUM."
(I AM A CITIZEN OF ROME.)

**Marcus Tullius Cicero (106–43BCE)**
*Roman politician and philosopher*

*Curia Julia, one of the meeting places of the Roman Senate*

### ROME'S PROTECTOR

Minerva, the goddess of wisdom and war, was first worshipped by the Etruscan people, who called her Menvra. She was said to look after the city of Rome in particular, but was worshipped all over the empire. Like her Greek equivalent, Athene, she is usually shown wearing armour and a helmet.

# REMEMBER ROME!

We remember Rome as one of the world's great civilizations. About 2,000 years ago the Romans ruled much of Europe, as well as western Asia and North Africa. We can still see the ruins of their great public buildings. We can imagine their splendid processions, their armies and epic battles, their feasts and chariot races, their slaves, emperors and struggles for power.

> By about 130CE, Rome was the largest city in the world, with a population of over a million.

www.roman-empire.net/children/index.html

Temple of Saturn

Temple of Antoninus Pius and Faustina

Temple of Castor and Pollux

## THE ETERNAL CITY

The Roman Forum, a public square at the heart of the city, was the hub of city life, a centre of commerce, government and religion. Remains of the ancient Forum still stand amidst the busy streets of modern Rome, over 2,700 years after the city was founded. Rome was already known as the eternal or everlasting city in ancient times.

### TRIUMPH OF POWER

This massive arch was built in honour of the military leader Titus after he captured the city of Jerusalem in 70CE and destroyed its great temple – mercilessly enforcing Roman power. Titus went on to become emperor from 79 to 81CE.

marble carved with images of Titus's victories

### THE PAST REVEALED

In 79CE the Roman town of Pompeii was buried by ash when the volcano Vesuvius erupted. Centuries later, its streets were uncovered by archaeologists, revealing how ordinary Romans lived their lives – cooking, shopping, scrawling graffiti on walls, working out at the public baths or visiting the theatre.

## RIVER OF THE ROMANS

Several ancient peoples – Umbrians, Etruscans, Sabines and Latins – lived close to the river Tiber during the Iron Age. But the river, an important route for trade at this time, is forever linked with the Romans, whose great city rose on its banks.

# SEVEN HILLS

## ETRUSCAN POWER

An Etruscan warrior goes to war. The Etruscans were one of many different peoples living in Italy. During the 6th century BCE they dominated Rome and many lands to the north as well. The Romans were greatly influenced by Etruscan technology, art and architecture.

Roman historians dated the foundation of their city to 753BCE. At that time the hills of central Italy, near the river Tiber, were occupied by small settlements of thatched huts, defended by bands of warriors. One of these settlements, on the Palatine Hill near the lowest crossing point of the Tiber, came to dominate its neighbours and became the city of Rome.

> Warriors in the hills used weapons made of iron, which began to be worked there between 900 and 700BCE.

*Romulus and Remus, legendary founders of Rome, are suckled by the she-wolf.*

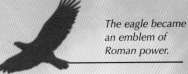

*The eagle became an emblem of Roman power.*

## HERO FROM TROY?

Nobody knows where the Romans first came from. Some stories say they were descended from Aeneas, a prince from Troy (in modern-day Turkey), who fled his city when it was burned down by the Greeks. After many adventures, Aeneas settled in Italy. DNA tests do suggest links between modern Italians and the region around Troy.

**Aeneas (in the centre of the picture) escaping from Troy**

"SO GREAT WAS THE EFFORT TO FOUND THE ROMAN NATION."

**Virgil (70–19BCE)**
*Roman poet, in The Aeneid, an epic poem about the adventures of Aeneas*

**the Lupercal cave in Rome (below), decorated in the reign of Augustus (27BCE–14CE) and rediscovered by archaeologists in 2007**

## RAISED BY WOLVES

Legends tell how Rome was founded by twin brothers called Romulus and Remus, sons of the war god Mars. As babies they were abandoned beside the Tiber, but were found by a wolf that looked after them. When the twins grew up, Remus was slain in a quarrel, and Romulus became the first king of Rome. The supposed wolf's cave, called the Lupercal, became a sacred place for the Romans.

**Samnite cavalry**

**Samnite infantry**

*Crests make the warrior look taller and scarier.*

*A breastplate is worn over a tunic.*

*This Samnite carries a round shield in the Greek style.*

# ROMAN REPUBLIC

The Romans fought their way to power, defeating other peoples living in Italy. They battled amongst themselves, too. In 510BCE they overthrew their king and Rome became a republic, governed by the Senate and popular assemblies which elected Rome's magistrates, including two consuls, or leaders. Patricians (noblemen) were still powerful. Ordinary citizens, called plebeians, had to struggle for their rights.

### S.P.Q.R.

Roman government was carried out in the name of the people. The initial letters S.P.Q.R. on items such as this battle standard stood for **S**enatus **P**opulus**q**ue **R**omanus – meaning 'the Senate and the People of Rome'.

## WARRING NEIGHBOURS

The Samnites were warriors, originally from the hills of southern Italy, who fought the Romans during three fierce wars between 343 and 290BCE. By about 250BCE, Rome had gained control over most of Italy, either by treaty or by military force.

> The Romans built the first paved roads across Italy to allow their armies to move quickly, so they could fight the Samnites.

*A pommel balances the blade of the sword (gladius).*

*Plates (bucculae) protect the cheeks.*

**The first Roman soldiers were property-owning citizens who provided their own armour.**

*The pilum (spear) could pierce enemy armour.*

www.schoolshistory.org.uk/republic.htm

## LOYAL SOLDIERS

At first, Roman soldiers were recruited for one campaign at a time. After 107BCE, the army became a professional, long-term fighting force. The Republican period was later known for its strong sense of duty and stern discipline.

**Roman helmet (galea)**

**short sword (gladius)**

## ● SAVED BY GEESE

In 390BCE Rome was attacked. The Gauls, a Celtic people, burned and looted much of the city, while the Romans took refuge on the Capitoline Hill. It was said that the Romans were alerted to the enemy's arrival when sacred geese, kept on the hill, began to cackle loudly.

# ANCIENT RELIGION

Throughout the year, Romans took part in festivals, sacrifices and religious rituals. Their religion developed out of a belief in spirits of the countryside and the home. It also took ideas of gods and goddesses from the Etruscans and from Greek settlers in Italy. The Romans made offerings and prayers to many different gods, and expected personal protection and favours in return.

## ROMAN TEMPLES

Splendid temples were built all over the empire, often by emperors or generals as thanksgiving for victory. Temples were centres of sacrifice and ritual. People did not go inside them to worship together.

a Roman temple in Syria

*Wine or incense would be offered at this shrine, called a lararium.*

## HOUSEHOLD GODS

Special gods looked after the home, the hearth and kitchen, as well as weddings and funerals. They were known as Lares and Penates. Each household had one Lar and two Penates, with their own shrines.

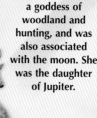

## GODS OF THE ROMAN STATE

Many gods and goddesses were officially worshipped as protectors of Roman cities, or of the state. In later days, the emperor served as high priest. Jupiter, Juno and Minerva (see page 4) were the chief gods and goddesses honoured in Rome.

Diana (left) was a goddess of woodland and hunting, and was also associated with the moon. She was the daughter of Jupiter.

Jupiter (left) was the greatest of the gods, a force of light, of thunder and lightning, and chief protector of the state.

Mars (left), originally a god of farming, was worshipped as the god of war. He was the father of Romulus and Remus.

Mercury (right) was the god of merchants and commerce, and was the messenger of the gods. He wore winged shoes.

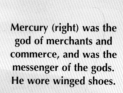 Roman priests tried to find out the intentions of the gods by studying the flight of birds.

# SACRIFICE OF A BULL

Important events and festivals were marked by sacrifices. Animals were killed as offerings, to please the gods and so prevent disasters. The choice of animal, the way it was killed and the examination of its intestines were very precise rituals. One mistake, and another sacrifice would have to be carried out in its place.

www.bbc.co.uk/schools/romans/religion.shtml

## KEY

1 priest carrying an offering of wine

2 altar, where organs of the sacred animal were burned

3 flamen, the senior priest, wearing a conical hat and laurel wreath

4 attendant, carrying the hammer used to kill the bull

5 haruspex, the priest who will inspect the bull's entrails

6 bull – a white bull was sacrificed to Jupiter or Mars

7 attendant catching the bull's blood

# ROME'S RIVAL

Rome had a powerful rival. The Phoenician port of Carthage, in North Africa, was the jewel in a ring of Phoenician colonies all around the Mediterranean Sea. Between 264 and 146BCE the Romans fought three Punic Wars in an attempt to crush their rivals. Thanks to a brilliant Carthaginian general, Hannibal, it was the Romans who were nearly defeated.

## THE CITY IN RUINS

Hannibal was finally defeated in Africa, at Zama, in 202BCE. Carthage itself remained a threat until in 146BCE the Romans razed it to the ground, burned its ships, and enslaved its people.

*Oarsmen toiled on benches below the deck.*

## ELEPHANT ARMY

In 218BCE Hannibal marched from Spain through Gaul, crossed the icy mountain passes of the Alps and invaded Italy. Amazingly, he brought his elephants, trained for battle, by this difficult route. Hannibal repeatedly defeated Roman armies, but failed to conquer Italy.

Roman ship

## BATTLE AT SEA

The Phoenicians were expert seafarers, and the Romans copied their ships. The warships were galleys, powered and steered by oars. The first Roman ships were fitted with a corvus, a spiked bridge which smashed on to the enemy deck, allowing marines to board. A pointed ram was used to hole the enemy's lead-covered hull.

> By 256BCE Carthage had a navy of about 350 warships.

Smaller ships supported the war galleys and kept them supplied.

Galleys could operate in shallow water.

"CARTHAGE MUST BE DESTROYED!"

**Cato the Elder (234–149 BCE)**
*Roman politician, who ended every speech in the Senate with these words*

Big, square sails were furled before battle.

**Carthaginian (Phoenician) ship**

www.historyworld.net/wrldhis/PlainTextHistories.asp?historyid=ac53

# HAIL, CAESAR!

Gaius Julius Caesar (100–44BCE) was a brilliant general. He conquered Gaul, invaded Britain and fought right across the Roman empire. He defeated his rivals in bitter civil wars. Military success brought him popularity and great political power, but this proved to be his undoing. Caesar's enemies complained that no single man should hold so much power in a republic. They plotted against him.

GAULS - Celtic tribes living in modern-day France, Belgium and the Alps

LEG XII

Caesar surrounded Alesia with a double circle of timber walls and towers.

The relief army of Gauls lies dead, or is carried off into slavery.

Vercingetorix lays down his sword and shield in surrender to Caesar. He was taken to Rome in chains and executed in 46BCE.

Julius Caesar was captured by pirates in 75BCE. Once freed, he had them all executed.

## THE HISTORY MAKER

Julius Caesar came from a noble family, which claimed descent from Aeneas himself. His life changed Roman history. His death was followed by civil war, and prepared the way for Rome to be ruled by emperors.

## CONQUEROR OF ALL

In this scene, Julius Caesar accepts the surrender of Vercingetorix, commander of the Gauls, at Alesia in 52BCE. The fort has been besieged, trapped within an iron ring of Roman troops. A huge army of Gauls has been slaughtered trying to break the siege. After a six-year campaign, heavily resisted by the Gauls, Caesar has finally won this province and all its riches for Rome.

*People from the fort are rounded up as prisoners, and disarmed.*

LEG VII

http://web.mac.com/heraklia/Caesar/index.html

## ☹ THE DOWNFALL

Would Julius Caesar become king? Republicans were enraged by the idea of anyone becoming this powerful. On 15 March 44BCE a group of conspirators, led by Marcus Junius Brutus and Gaius Cassius Longinus, attacked him in Rome. He died from 23 stab wounds.

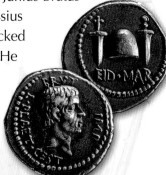

**a coin marking the assassination of Caesar (Brutus on one side, daggers on the other)**

# RISE OF THE EMPIRE

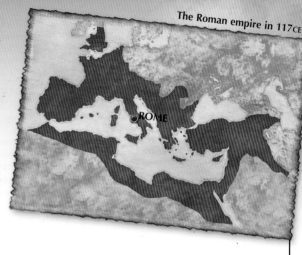

The Roman empire in 117CE

ROME

The murder of Julius Caesar did not mark a return to republican government after all. After years of strife, it was Caesar's great-nephew (and adopted son), Octavian, who came to rule Rome in 27BCE. His new title was Imperator Caesar Augustus. Augustus did not abolish the republic, but simply took over more and more public offices for himself. Soon the Senate was losing any real power. Rome's future belonged to its emperors.

## RULING FROM ROME

Rome was becoming the hub of a great empire. What happened there affected not only people in Italy, but Britons, Gauls, Germans, Greeks, Phoenicians, Iberians, Africans and Asians. Rome even made contact with the emperors of China.

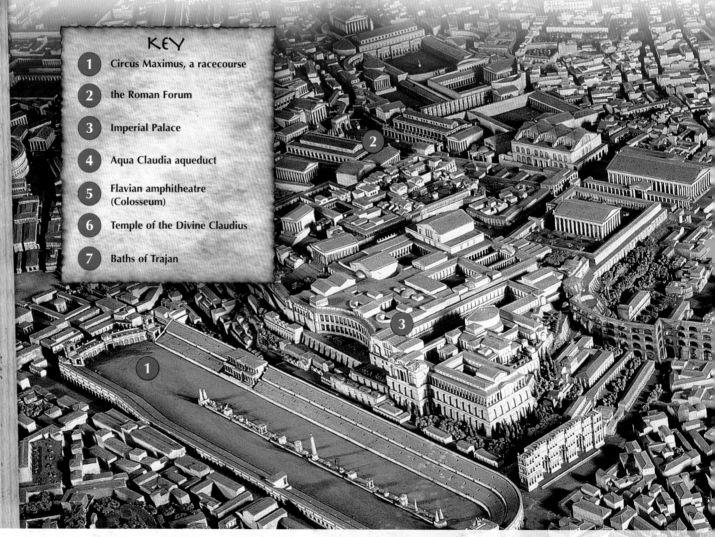

### KEY

1. Circus Maximus, a racecourse
2. the Roman Forum
3. Imperial Palace
4. Aqua Claudia aqueduct
5. Flavian amphitheatre (Colosseum)
6. Temple of the Divine Claudius
7. Baths of Trajan

> More than a billion (1,000,000,000) litres of water had to be channelled into Rome each day.

# ✪ THE COLOUR OF POWER

A type of sea snail called the murex provided a reddish-purple dye, which was first traded by the Phoenicians. The dye was very expensive, so the colour became a symbol of royalty or nobility in the ancient world. In Rome, the colour purple was reserved for emperors.

**murex shell**

"HE COULD BOAST THAT HE INHERITED IT BRICK AND LEFT IT MARBLE."

**Suetonius (c. 69–c. 130CE)**

*Roman historian, describing Emperor Augustus's improvements to Rome*

http://resourcesforhistory.com/map.htm

## A SPLENDID CITY

Every emperor wanted to leave his mark on Rome in the form of fine new public buildings, gleaming with marble. To a slave arriving from northern Europe, the sight must have been incredible. The capital had racecourses, temples, theatres, law courts, public baths, busy markets and grand palaces.

TAXATION – money collected from the public for use by the government

# ROMAN WORLD

The Roman empire at its largest stretched from the coast of what is now Portugal to Iraq, from the Scottish borders to Morocco, from Romania to Egypt. Along its dusty roads tramped the legions, enforcing Roman rule. On its rivers and seas sailed merchant ships, trading in grain, oil, wine, olives, marble, metals, glass, pottery, textiles – and slaves. This vast area used the same currency, with coins of bronze, silver and gold.

### NORTHERN LANDS

Roman-occupied Britain (Britannia) exported woollen cloaks, hunting dogs, lead and silver.

The Roman empire spanned snowy moorlands, fertile river valleys and hot deserts (right).

### RIVER DANUBE

The Danube, stretching from Germany to the Black Sea, formed an important border, and forts were built along it.

## ● MADE IN THE EMPIRE

The Romans were great craft workers, and also learned new skills from peoples they conquered. They imported glass from western Asia and Egypt. Pottery was made in Italy and in Gaul, where red pottery dishes known as 'Samian ware' were produced for export. Roman goldsmiths crafted fine jewellery, inlaid with precious stones.

gold 'snake' armband

glass jug

Wine and olive oil were transported and stored in amphorae (pottery jars with handles). They are sometimes brought to light when Roman shipwrecks are discovered.

# SOUTH TO EGYPT

Egypt's civilization was already thousands of years old when it became part of the Roman empire in 30BCE. The Romans profited from taxation and from the grain grown in the Nile valley.

Roman tourists came to marvel at ancient Egyptian monuments, such as the Pyramids of Giza.

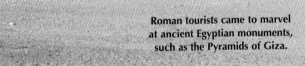

mosaics showing merchant ships from Ostia, the ancient port of Rome

## LUSH VINEYARDS

The Romans were expert growers of the grape vine. They brought their skills from Italy to many parts of the empire, and often planted vineyards on sunny hillsides.

## TRADING ROUTES

Trading routes extended overland through Asia and Africa. They connected with seaports around the Mediterranean and the Black Sea. A sea voyage from southern Spain to Italy took about nine days, while Egypt to Italy could take about 15.

*The channel runs slightly downhill so that the water flows easily.*

*This section of the channel is enclosed, for the water. It will be lined with cement.*

## THE AQUEDUCT

Labourers haul, heave and sweat. Masons chip at great blocks of stone. Carpenters build timber frames and scaffolding. The new aqueduct will carry a supply of spring water from the hills to a nearby city. High arches are needed to support the aqueduct as it crosses a river valley.

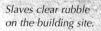

*Slaves clear rubble on the building site.*

# BUILDING IN STONE

The Romans were a practical people. The success of their empire depended on technology and engineering, on roads, bridges, dams, drains, mines, millstones and cranes. They learned how to build stone arches from the Etruscans, and how to build waterwheels from the Greeks and Asians. Their own brilliant invention was Roman concrete, made from a special type of cement.

 ❯ Roman cranes were often powered by treadwheels, turned by tramping slaves.

### STAYING POWER

This fine Roman aqueduct is the Pont du Gard in southern France. It is 49m high and 275m long. It has survived nearly 2,000 years. Hundreds of other examples of Roman engineering can still be seen throughout the old empire.

## ⊖ ALL ROADS LEAD TO ROME

The Romans built long, straight highways from place to place. Routes were carefully surveyed and the roads were well paved and drained, and built on firm foundations. The road network provided fast communications across the empire, encouraged trade and allowed the rapid movement of troops.

paving stones on the Appian Way, Rome's most important road

Cranes with treadwheels could lift much heavier loads than cranes with winches.

The piers rise from rock in the river bed.

**"GLORIA EXERCITUS"**
**(GLORY TO THE ARMY)**

**wording on many Roman coins**

*Dacians fought with swords, battle scythes, spears, bows and arrows.*

# BATTLE HONOURS

Dacians fight like cornered wolves as Roman legions steadily advance. Dacia was the part of eastern Europe now known as Romania and Moldova. In 85–86, 101–102 and 105–106CE it was repeatedly ravaged by war. Rome was victorious, winning control of the region's rich gold mines. Thousands of Dacians were sent back to Rome as slaves.

**signum (battle standard)**

**Dacian warrior**

> In 9CE three whole Roman legions were defeated and destroyed in a single battle in Germany.

# LEGIONS AT WAR

The Roman army, ruthless, well-trained and disciplined, seemed unstoppable. It was usually divided into fighting units called legions, each made up of some 5,500 men. Legions were supported by cavalry and non-Roman troops called auxiliaries. A soldier's life was tough. He might have to march over 30km a day, carrying tools and food rations as well as sword, shield and spears.

### STORY IN STONE

Trajan's Column in Rome dates from 113CE. It pictures scenes from Roman victories in the Dacian wars. From these we can learn about details of Roman armour, hand weapons, catapults, bridge building, forts and ships.

www.caerleon.net/history/army/page2.html

*A fighting unit of about 80 soldiers was called a century.*

*Roman reserves wait to join the battle.*

*Segmented armour is made up of metal plates.*

scutum (shield)

LIMES – the Latin word for a frontier region in the Roman empire (the plural is limites)

# FRONTIER FIGHTING

Once a land had been conquered by the legions, it had to be held secure. The empire's many frontiers, called limites, ran across northern Britain, down the rivers Rhine and Danube, and through the deserts of Arabia and North Africa. The frontiers were heavily defended with forts, military camps, walls, earthworks, beacons and watchtowers. Over the years, they also became routes for trade and communications.

A centurion takes his orders for the day

a legion's standard, the aquila or eagle

gatehouse

## KEY

1 fortified gates on each side

2 barracks (soldiers' living quarters, coloured blue)

3 grain stores

4 hospital block

5 principia (headquarters)

6 praetorium (commander's house)

A sentry guards Arbeia fort, built beside the River Tyne in northern Britain, in about 160CE. This military base supplied 17 forts along Hadrian's Wall, the northern frontier of the Roman empire.

> A colonia was a town built on conquered lands – such as Cologne in Germany.

Housesteads, a stone fort on Hadrian's Wall built in 124CE, is a typical frontier fort.

outer wall

1
2
3
4
5
6
1
2
1

## INSIDE A FORT

Forts along Hadrian's Wall were garrisoned (manned and defended) by Roman troops and foreign auxiliaries. The troops slept eight to a room in long barrack blocks. There was a bath house, and communal toilets with drains. Daily orders were issued from the principia, or headquarters. Outside the fort was a village with bars, shops and civilians' houses.

### HOME FROM HOME

The commander of a Roman fort expected all the comforts his high rank could bring. He and his wife might demand underfloor heating, a luxurious dining room, baths, domestic slaves and the best imported wine. He wanted to show off Roman civilization to the local barbarians.

*training in use of the sword and shield*

### TRAINING AND DUTIES

In times of peace, troops needed to stay fit and keep disciplined. They were given training, drill, marching and patrols. Off duty, many had local girlfriends. Sometimes they married them when they left the army.

## LIFE ON THE FRONTIER

off duty: dicing and gaming

Writing tablets found at the Vindolanda fort on Hadrian's Wall tell us how people lived. They mention hunting and pay, supplies of barley, pork, oysters and the local beer. One letter asks for woolly socks and underpants to be sent to keep out the cold. Another is an invitation to a birthday party given by a lady called Claudia Severa.

letter from Vindolanda (from around 79–105CE)

# A DAY IN THE COUNTRY

VILLA - a large house in the countryside, often with estates used for farming

Many soldiers dreamed of retiring to the countryside and owning a farm. There they could grow a few crops, raise cattle or keep bees or geese. Rich people owned big country houses, called villas. These had large agricultural estates, which provided grain, fruit, meat and wool for the empire. The land belonging to the villa was managed by bailiffs and worked by slaves.

Bunches of grapes were harvested in baskets and then trodden underfoot or crushed in a wine press. The juice was then fermented and aged. Wine was stored in sealed pottery jars.

Grain could be ground into flour in a quern, or hand mill, made up of two round stones.

a press for making olive oil

a columbarium or dovecote

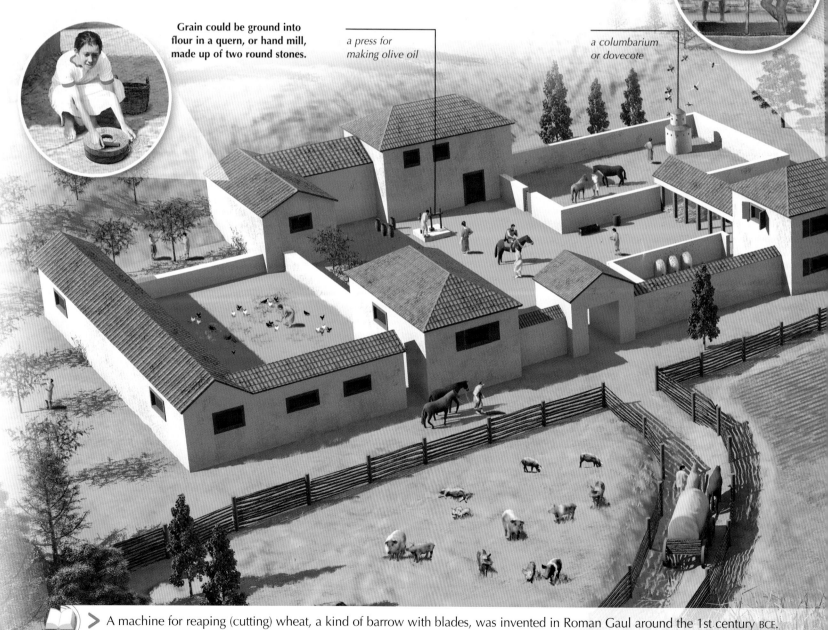

> A machine for reaping (cutting) wheat, a kind of barrow with blades, was invented in Roman Gaul around the 1st century BCE.

**Hadrian's villa included beautiful pools, columns, statues and mosaics.**

### LUXURY RETREAT

One of the grandest villas was built by the emperor Hadrian at Tibur (Tivoli). It was a refuge from the hustle and bustle of Rome, but was more a palace than a country house, being made up of over 30 buildings.

# THE FERTILE LAND

Roman farmers needed to grow large amounts of wheat and barley to feed the people in the towns and cities. They grew cabbages, peas and beans, hay and other crops to feed the animals. The Romans knew how to care for the soil by using manure and varying the crops.

www.whitehallvilla.co.uk

*An orchard provided fruit.*

*Wheat was generally harvested with sickles.*

*Rivers and lakes provided fish and waterfowl.*

*A slave looks after the sheep.*

*A plough is drawn by two oxen.*

### ACROSS THE EMPIRE

This mosaic from Algeria, in North Africa, shows grape vines being tended. There were villas and farming estates across the empire. Produce varied with the land and climate. The Romans introduced more than 50 new food plants to Britain alone.

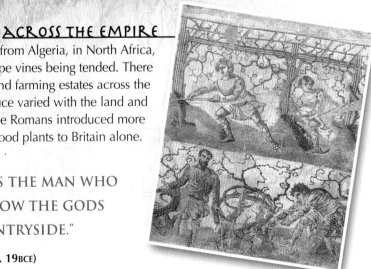

"FORTUNATE TOO IS THE MAN WHO HAS COME TO KNOW THE GODS OF THE COUNTRYSIDE."

**Virgil (70–c. 19BCE)**

*Roman poet*

# CITY STREETS

Roman cities were surrounded by walls, and had public gates and paved roads for the traffic going in and out. In Rome itself and in other big cities there were large apartment blocks, called insulae, as well as town houses large and small. These had only small shuttered windows and wooden doors facing the street. Streets were noisy with the cries of shopkeepers, market traders and rumbling cartwheels.

## STROLL BACK IN TIME

You can wander today through the streets of Pompeii and Herculaneum, near Naples, Italy. These towns were buried by the eruption of Vesuvius in 79CE. There, it is easy to imagine how the Romans lived, traded and entertained themselves.

*The latest shipment of slaves goes on sale.*

## ⊖ ROMAN SLAVES

Around one-third of the population may have been slaves. Brought from all over the empire, slaves were owned by their master, could be bought and sold, and had no rights. Some worked as household servants, tutors, labourers or miners. They might be freed as a reward for good service.

**This tag, worn by a slave, asks the public to return him to his owner if he runs away.**

*A Greek tutor takes his pupils to class.*

busy market stalls

> Augustus set up a body of firefighters and watchmen to protect Rome.

## A CITY CORNER

This corner of the city, a little way from the centre, is linked by main road to the forum, which is where the public buildings, temples and central markets are located. Here the morning's activities are getting under way. Shops are open. A wealthy patrician talks with his wife in his garden, while his daughter is carried by litter to visit relatives.

www.historyforkids.org/learn/romans/architecture/houses/houses.htm

shop selling hot food

stepping stones

A thief runs off with some fruit.

shop selling cloth

patrician's courtyard garden

# A DINNER INVITATION

"SCALE RED MULLET AND PUT THEM IN A CLEAN PAN... ADD OLIVE OIL AND HEAT... ADD HONEY WINE, SPRINKLE WITH PEPPER AND SERVE."

**Apicius**
*in* De Re Coquinaria *(a famous Roman cookery book)*

The main meal of the Roman day, cena, was eaten in the early evening, perhaps outside during the summer. For the wealthy, it was often a splendid affair. The indoor dining room of a villa or town house would be beautifully decorated. It was called the triclinium. People lay on couches, arranged around three sides of a low table, to eat. Three courses were normal, but for a banquet there might be seven or eight.

*A lightweight dining gown is called a synthesis.*

*Dancers and musicians might entertain guests between courses.*

## DINNER PARTY

Remove your sandals when you arrive, and slaves will wash your feet. Now take your couch. Shellfish to start with? Songbirds, snails or dormice? Perhaps hare, wild boar, calf's brains or venison for the main course, with peas or asparagus? And finish with figs and honey cakes.

At the winter festival of Saturnalia, masters would wait on their slaves in a special banquet.

## THE KITCHEN

Ovens were wood-fired. Meat could be roasted on a spit, or boiled or stewed in iron pots. Oil and wine were stored in pottery amphorae (jars). Many of the saucepans, frying pans and griddles looked like the ones we use today.

www.bbc.co.uk/history/ancient/romans/recipes.shtml

## ● A TASTE OF ROME

A Roman cookery book by Apicius has survived, telling us that Roman food was highly seasoned with herbs and spices. It was cooked in olive oil and often served with sauces made from honey, vinegar, wine or garum (a salty pickle made from fish guts – a bit like modern Thai fish sauce).

**Sauce made from fish was a vital ingredient in Roman cookery.**

# FASHION AND STYLE

TOGA – a heavy woollen robe, cut in a semi-circle, folded and draped over the body

By the 2nd century CE, rich women's hair styles had become very elaborate. Many women curled and bleached their hair. Some wore hair extensions or wigs.

All Roman clothes were based on the simple tunic. Slaves and working people wore a cheap, practical version of this garment. A wealthy Roman citizen would wear a short linen tunic beneath a long robe called a toga. The ladies of his family would wear an under-tunic with a long, high-waisted over-tunic or dress called a stola. Sometimes they would cover this with a shawl, called a palla, draped over their shoulders or head.

The glitter of gold and the sheen of mother-of-pearl made this necklace a desirable item in first-century Pompeii.

## LUCKY LOCKET

The bulla might be made of leather, cloth or gold.

Each Roman child was given a locket at birth. Called a bulla, it was worn around the neck at all times. It contained an amulet or good-luck charm, and was worn until the child was grown-up (for girls, this was when they married).

*make-up casket*

*Venus, goddess of love, makes herself beautiful.*

## CHANGING CLOTH

Women enjoyed different colours and styles, and liked to keep up with changes in the fabrics available: moving from wool to linen or cotton and later even to expensive imported silk. Men's woollen togas were often too bulky for comfort. After about 100CE they became smaller and more lightweight.

### PREPARING FOR A PARTY

A wealthy woman would spend hours getting ready for a party. Her slaves would bring mirrors, hairpins, perfumes and oils. Cosmetics included pale face-powder made from chalk or (poisonous) lead, and lipstick made from red ochre.

One emperor even got his nickname because as a child he wore a certain style of boots: Caligula means 'little army boots'.

## THE PURPLE STRIPE

*a leading citizen*

Dress showed a person's rank in society. Any free-born Roman citizen could wear a plain white toga, although he might not do so every day. Boys under the age of 16 wore the toga with a purple stripe, and important people also wore a stripe as adults. A broad purple stripe was worn by senators only.

*A traveller wears a practical woollen cloak.*

### WARM AND DRY

Woollen cloaks and capes, often with hoods, were worn by men and women to keep warm and stay dry. Farm workers in muddy fields might also bind their legs with strips of cloth, and soldiers wore breeches under their tunics.

### STEPPING OUT

Skilled cobblers made footwear for all purposes. Romans wore light leather sandals indoors, and stouter shoes or sandals outdoors. Calf-length boots might be worn by huntsmen or army officers. Military footwear had studded soles.

a Roman woman wearing a stola and her husband wearing a tunic and everyday toga

# STAGE & ARENA

Roman entertainment included music, singing, dance and theatre. Romans also loved to play dice and watch horse races or boxing. Then, in amphitheatres such as Rome's Colosseum, there were gladiator fights: violent shows where packed crowds watched trained combatants fight, sometimes to the death.

AMPHITHEATRE – *a circular or oval stadium – the word means 'double-theatre'*

### ACTING A PART

Romans took their ideas about drama from the Greeks. Comedies were very popular. Actors wore masks to represent the characters they played. Dramas were staged in large open-air theatres.

## DIE, GLADIATOR!

Gladiators were divided into various types, according to their armour, helmet, or the weapons they used. They fought one pair at a time, and each type usually fought another particular type, although this scene imagines several fighting at once. The bravest gladiators were very popular with the crowds, and could win a lot of prize money.

retarius

Thracian

In 107CE 5,000 pairs of gladiators took part in the biggest ever session of combat.

SPQR

murmillo

*The name 'gladiator' means swordsman.*

*A greave (ocrea) protected the leg.*

secutor

**Arena was the Latin word for sand. The combat area was filled with sand to soak up the blood. It was freshly raked after each contest.**

*Many gladiators met an early death in the arena.*

# ⊖ THRILLS AND SPILLS AT THE RACES

four-horse chariot (quadriga)

The Circus Maximus was Rome's great race track, and could seat over 150,000 spectators. Here people could place their bets, watch chariots thunder around the track and cheer on their team (Reds, Greens, Blues or Whites). They watched jockeys risk their lives by jumping from horse to horse or leaping over chariots.

triumphal arch

The emperor rides
in a golden chariot.

# EMPERORS

The emperor claimed to be just another Roman
citizen, a 'first among equals'. In fact, he had immense
personal power. Usually the emperor passed his
wealth and position on to an adopted son and heir.
But power was sometimes seized by successful military
commanders. Emperors were protected by soldiers of
the Praetorian Guard, but lived in constant fear of
betrayal, political plots, assassins and poisoners.

Prisoners of war
are paraded through
Rome's streets.

 Roman emperors wore a laurel wreath, an ancient emblem of victory, as a crown.

# TRAJAN'S TRIUMPH

A triumph was the public celebration of a major military victory. It was marked by an extravagant procession through Rome, and feasting, games and gladiator shows. Trajan's triumph in 107CE lasted 123 days, and celebrated his victories in the Dacian wars. Spanish-born Trajan was a popular emperor, who reigned from 98 to 117CE.

relatives and friends of the emperor

oxen for sacrifice to the gods

spoils of war

# THE GOOD, THE BAD AND THE MAD

Some Roman emperors were wise or successful rulers, but others were bad, incompetent or insane. It became the custom to declare emperors gods once they had died.

**Caligula (reigned 37–41CE)** was known as cruel and mad – he even tried to make his horse consul of Rome. The stories were probably exaggerated by his enemies.

**Claudius (reigned 41–54CE)** may have suffered from cerebral palsy. He was interested in law and history, and was an effective ruler. He possibly died by poisoning.

**Nero (reigned 54–68CE)** has gone down in history as a brutal tyrant. He was declared an enemy of the state by the Senate and forced to commit suicide.

**Hadrian (reigned 76–138CE)** served as a soldier before becoming emperor. He was interested in architecture, Latin and Greek poetry, and philosophy.

**Marcus Aurelius (reigned, partly as joint emperor, 161–180CE)** was a wise ruler and military leader. He wrote, in Greek, a great book of philosophy called *Meditations*.

**Constantine I (reigned 306–337CE)** was the first Roman emperor to become a Christian. He built a new imperial capital at Byzantium (Constantinople, modern-day Istanbul).

# NEW RELIGIONS

As the empire grew, Romans encountered many different peoples, with their own religious beliefs and customs. Some foreign gods seemed very similar to the early Greek and Roman ones, and appealed to the Romans. These were tolerated, and sometimes Romans even made them part of their culture. However, wherever religious beliefs clashed with the Roman way of doing things, or stirred up political opposition, there was trouble. At times Jews and Christians were persecuted by the Roman state.

The worship of Isis attracted many Roman women. She was associated with childbirth.

## MYSTERIES OF ISIS

Isis, a mother-goddess of ancient Egypt, came to be worshipped by large numbers of Romans, from slaves to members of the imperial family. Isis-worship was a 'mystery cult', so its rituals were secret, known only to its followers. Women played an important part in Roman Isis-worship.

jangling bronze pins

The sistrum, a sacred musical rattle, was one of the objects used by priests and priestesses of Isis.

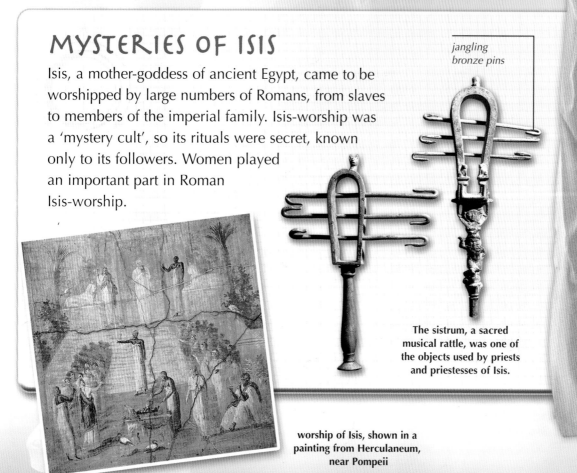

worship of Isis, shown in a painting from Herculaneum, near Pompeii

> Nero blamed Christians for the Great Fire of Rome in 64CE. Many were put to death.

www.roman-empire.net/children/gods.html

## IN THE LAND OF DRUIDS

The Roman invasion of Britain was opposed by Britain's Celtic priests, called druids. The Romans attacked the druids' holy island of Mona (Anglesey, or Ynys Môn, in Wales), burning down its sacred groves of oak trees. Later, the Romans merged many Celtic gods with their own. Sulis, goddess of the springs at Bath in south-west England, came to be linked with the Roman goddess Minerva.

**a bronze statue of Sulis-Minerva**

*The Greek letters chi and rho identify the figure as Christ.*

**This 4th-century mosaic of Christ was found in a Roman villa.**

## CHRIST, THE SON OF GOD

Jesus Christ was crucified in Jersualem, on Roman orders, in about 30CE. His followers, Christians, believed he was the Son of God and that he rose from the dead. The early Christians were persecuted by Rome, but in 313CE they were given the right to worship freely. By the end of the century, Christianity had become the dominant religion of the empire.

**ruins of a mithraeum in northern Britain**

*Mithras slays a bull. Corn and all life were believed to flow from the bull's blood.*

## THE BULL-SLAYER

The worship of the god Mithras became increasingly popular under the empire. The cult, which involved frightening initiation ceremonies, combined Persian imagery with ideas drawn from astrology, and worshippers met regularly to eat and drink together. These all-male secret rituals took place in a darkened cave-like temple, the mithraeum.

BARBARIAN – the Roman word for peoples from outside the empire

"HE EMBELLISHED IT WITH
VERY MANY PLACES OF WORSHIP,
VERY LARGE SHRINES, AND
SPLENDID HOUSES."

**Eusebius of Caesarea (c. 263–339CE)**
*writing about Constantine founding Constantinople in 330CE*

The great Byzantine church
of Hagia Sophia (built
532–537CE) is still part
of the Istanbul skyline.

# WEST AND EAST

Ruling the vast empire from Rome was never
easy. There were rebellions and rivalries. In 286CE
reforms brought in by the emperor Diocletian
led to a division of the empire between west and
east. This became permanent from 395CE, with
Constantinople (modern Istanbul) becoming the
eastern capital. Western Goths sacked Rome in
410. By 476 the power of the western Roman
emperors had faded. The world was changing.

### CONSTANTINE THE GREAT

Constantinople was named after
Constantine I. He was proclaimed
emperor by the legions in Britain
in 306CE and went on to become
the first Christian ruler of the
Roman empire, both west and east

### NEW DEFENCES

Roman Britain, in the
western empire, came
under attack from Saxon
raiders. A chain of forts
was built around the
south-east coast to
defend the province.

 > The last emperor to rule in the west was a teenager called Romulus, like Rome's legendary founder.

## ATTACKS ON ROME

Roman legions battle with Goths in 250CE. These northern 'barbarians', a group of Germanic peoples, grew more powerful. The limites were overrun by hostile armies and by 401 the legions had to be withdrawn from Britain to meet this threat.

## ☻ BURIED TREASURE

By about 350CE many northern parts of the empire were no longer secure places to live. One family threatened by raiders at Mildenhall in Britain buried their silver to prevent it falling into the wrong hands – and never recovered it. Thirty-four beautiful plates, dishes, spoons and goblets were discovered in 1943.

www.historyforkids.org/learn/romans/history/Fall.htm

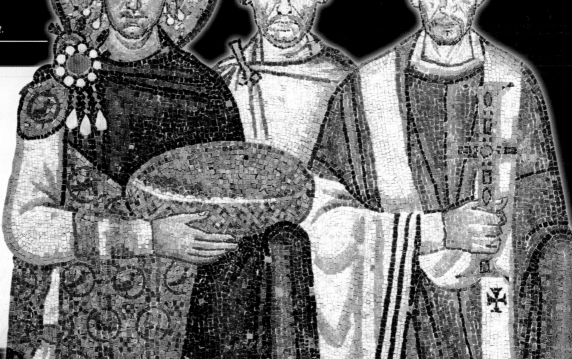

*Justinian ruled the Byzantine (eastern) empire from 527 to 565. He was a famous law-maker who recaptured many lands in the west.*

# EASTERN EMPIRE

Rome survived in the east as the Byzantine empire, and thrived for another thousand years. Constantinople was the centre of the eastern (orthodox) Christian faith, and became a centre of trade with Asia. The city fell to the Ottoman Turks in 1453.

# ROME LIVES ON

GERMANIC – *belonging to a group of northern European peoples, including Angles, Saxons, Franks, Vandals and Goths*

"WHILE STANDS THE COLOSSEUM, ROME SHALL STAND; WHEN FALLS THE COLOSSEUM, ROME SHALL FALL; AND WHEN ROME FALLS – THE WORLD."

**Lord Byron (1788–1824)**
*English poet, in the poem* Childe Harold's Pilgrimage

The Byzantine emperors failed to hold on to Rome's lands in the west. Much of the old empire came under the rule of Germanic kings. One of these, the Frankish ruler Charlemagne, created a new 'Holy Roman empire' in 800. The city of Rome remained the headquarters of the Catholic church. This ensured that it kept great political power and influence for hundreds of years.

## THE ROMAN CHURCH

The Roman Catholic church dominated the lives of people in western Europe throughout the Middle Ages. The church used the Romans' language. Official documents were in Latin, and scholars wrote and studied in Latin. For centuries afterwards, scientists and scholars wrote in Latin rather than their own languages.

*Medieval scriptures (church writings) were copied in Latin.*

**Scientists still use Latin for the official names of plants and animals and many other scientific terms.**

*This botanical illustration includes the plant's Latin name at its base.*

> Catalan, French, Italian, Spanish, Portuguese and Romanian are just some of the languages descended from Latin.

# ROME ALL AROUND US

The Roman style of architecture, which includes buildings with tall columns or impressive domes, became very popular again in Europe from about the 16th century onwards. Many grand public buildings are built in the Roman or 'neoclassical' style. Modern legal systems, too, have been influenced by the laws of the Roman and Byzantine empires. Many parliaments are still called 'Senate', like that of ancient Rome. Thousands of years after Rome was founded, it still affects our daily lives.

the Parliament of the European Union, which reunites many of the old parts of the Roman empire

The US Capitol in Washington D.C. includes the Senate and the House of Representatives. It is built in a neoclassical style.

www.bbc.co.uk/history/ancient/romans/tech_01.shtml

## NEW EMPERORS

During the French Revolution (1789–1799) many people took Republican Rome as their ideal. When Napoleon became emperor of France in 1804, he adopted symbols of the Roman empire, such as wreaths and eagles.

## ANCIENT ROME TODAY

Tourists admire the Colosseum in Rome, and imagine the gladiators fighting and the roar of the crowd. All over the old empire there are fascinating reminders of the past, from forts and temples to public baths and aqueducts.

The heart of ancient Rome is recreated for television.

## BRINGING ROME BACK TO LIFE

Mobile telephones and sound recording equipment? Can this be ancient Rome? Actors take a break between filming scenes from *Rome*. This successful television series was shot in Italy – much of it in Rome itself – in 2005–2007. Films, television programmes and novels all ensure that the Roman age is kept alive in our imagination.

# GLOSSARY

## ARCHAEOLOGY

The study of the past, using scientific examination of remains and ruins, carried out by archaeologists.

## ARENA

The sand-covered area in an amphitheatre, where shows were staged.

## ASSASSINATE

To murder a public figure, often for political reasons.

## AUXILIARY

In a supporting role. Foreign auxiliary troops often fought alongside the Roman legions.

## BARRACKS

Accommodation for soldiers in a fort.

## BULLA

A lucky charm or amulet, worn around the neck by Roman children.

## BYZANTINE EMPIRE

The empire that grew out of the eastern division of the Roman empire. Its capital, Constantinople, was on the site of ancient Byzantium (modern Istanbul).

## CAVALRY

Troops mounted on horseback.

## CELTS

A group of ancient European peoples who by early Roman times were living in Britain, Ireland, France, southern and western Germany, Spain, northern Italy and Turkey.

## CENTURION

A senior army officer, in charge of centuries (units of 60 to 80 men) or larger units within a cohort of about 480 men.

## CHARIOT

A lightweight, horse-drawn two-wheeled cart, used for racing or warfare.

## CIVIL WAR

A war fought between two groups from the same country.

## CONSUL

One of the two joint leaders of the Roman republic, elected each year by an assembly of mostly wealthy and powerful Romans. Under the empire, consuls still existed, but they had little real power.

## DACIANS

A people of Thracian origin, who in ancient times inhabited an area that is mostly now covered by Romania, including the lower Danube valley and the Carpathian mountains.

## EMPEROR

The ruler of an empire.

## FORUM

The centre of business, trade, government and religion in an ancient Roman town.

## FRONTIER

A border between nations or regions. The frontier of the Roman empire was called the limes (plural: limites).

## GALLEY

A large ship powered by sails and oars.

## GLADIATOR

A trained fighter who engages in mortal combat to entertain a crowd.

## GOTHS

A group of Germanic tribes who invaded the lands of the Roman empire. They included eastern Goths (Ostrogoths) and western Goths (Visigoths).

## LATIN

The chief language of Rome and its empire. The earliest inhabitants of Rome were the Latin people, a tribe from the region of Latium, the area surrounding Rome.

## LEGION

The most important fighting unit within the Roman army. At different periods its numbers varied from about 4,500 to 5,200 soldiers.

## LITTER

A platform, carried by hand, used to carry wealthy passengers in Roman times.

## MOSAIC

A picture made up from coloured fragments of pottery, glass or stone.

## PATRICIAN

A member of one of the ancient aristocratic families of Rome.

## PERSECUTE

To oppress or harm a person or group of people, most commonly on account of their race, religion or political views.

## PHOENICIANS

People of the Phoenician civilization of the eastern Mediterranean, famed for its seafaring, trading and colonies.

## PLEBEIAN

Belonging to the ordinary families of Roman birth, rather than to the upper or patrician class.

## REPUBLIC

A state ruled by the people or their representatives, rather than by a king, queen or emperor.

## RITUALS

Formal actions which are performed in a particular, solemn way, often as part of religious worship or public ceremonies.

## SENATE

The governing assembly of ancient Rome, chosen from leading citizens. It advised the consuls, who could pass laws.

## SENTRY

A soldier whose duty is to stand guard and keep watch.

## SHRINE

A place that is considered holy because it is associated with a sacred object, person or god. Roman households each had a shrine to their family gods, called a lararium.

## SIEGE

The surrounding of a city by an army, with the aim of cutting off its supplies and forcing it to surrender.

## SLAVE

Someone who is deprived of his or her freedom and rights and forced to work for no reward.

## TEMPLE

A building dedicated to a god or goddess, used for rituals, festivals or offerings.

## TRIUMPH

A grand ceremonial parade held in Rome to honour a victorious general or emperor.

## WRITING TABLET

A wooden board used for writing. It was often covered in wax which could be marked by a point or stylus, and then smoothed out to be reused.

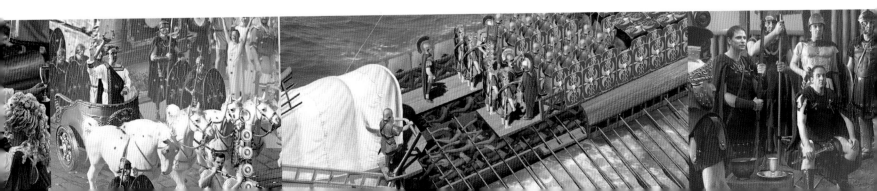

# INDEX

# INVESTIGATE

Get in touch with the past by visiting archaeological sites or museums. Read some ancient Roman writers (in English), or cook a Roman meal!

the Roman baths and museum at Bath, England

## MUSEUMS AND EXHIBITIONS

All over Great Britain there are local museums with real Roman coins, weapons and statues. These help you to imagine what it was like to be a Roman soldier or a slave.

 *The British Museum Pocket Timeline of Ancient Rome* (British Museum Press)

 The Roman Baths at Bath, Abbey Church Yard, Bath BA1 1LZ, UK

www.britishmuseum.org

a wall-painting excavated in Pompeii, Italy

## ARCHAEOLOGY

Roman forts, amphitheatres, baths, villas and temples can be visited at home or abroad. Many archaeological finds from excavations at Roman sites tell us fascinating details of everyday life in ancient times.

 *Pompeii* by Richard Platt and Manuela Cappon (Kingfisher)

 The Museum of London, London Wall, London EC2Y 5HN, UK

www.britarch.ac.uk/yac  and  www.channel4.com/history/microsites/B/bigromandig

the character of Flavia in the Children's BBC TV adaptation of the *Roman Mysteries* books

## ART AND FICTION

Novels set in Rome are always popular, and Roman mythology has some great stories, too. If you are interested in art, original mosaics and wall paintings have survived and can be seen at some museums.

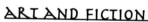 *The Orchard Book of Roman Myths* by Geraldine McCaughrean and Emma Chichester Clark (Orchard)

 The Roman Painted House at Dover, New Street, Dover, Kent CT17 9AJ, UK

www.romanmysteries.com/indexflash.htm

ruins of the Roman Library of Celsus in Ephesus, Turkey

## ROMAN BUILDINGS

Find out about old Roman buildings near you. What were they made of? How were they different from Roman buildings in Rome itself, or other parts of the empire?

 *Rome in Spectacular Cross-section* by Stephen Biesty (Oxford University Press)

 Fishbourne Roman palace, Salthill Road, Fishbourne, Chichester, West Sussex, PO19 3QR, UK

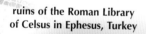 www.vindolanda.com

Bull Terrier          Chinese Crested          Bulldog          Dalmatian

For El

# DOGS

## Emily Gravett

MACMILLAN CHILDREN'S BOOKS

I love dogs.

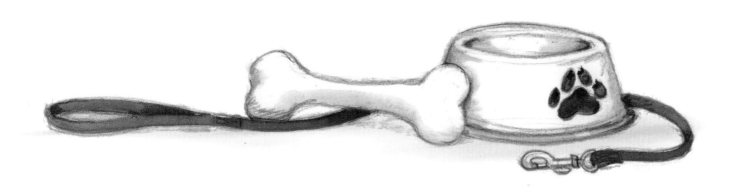

I love big dogs

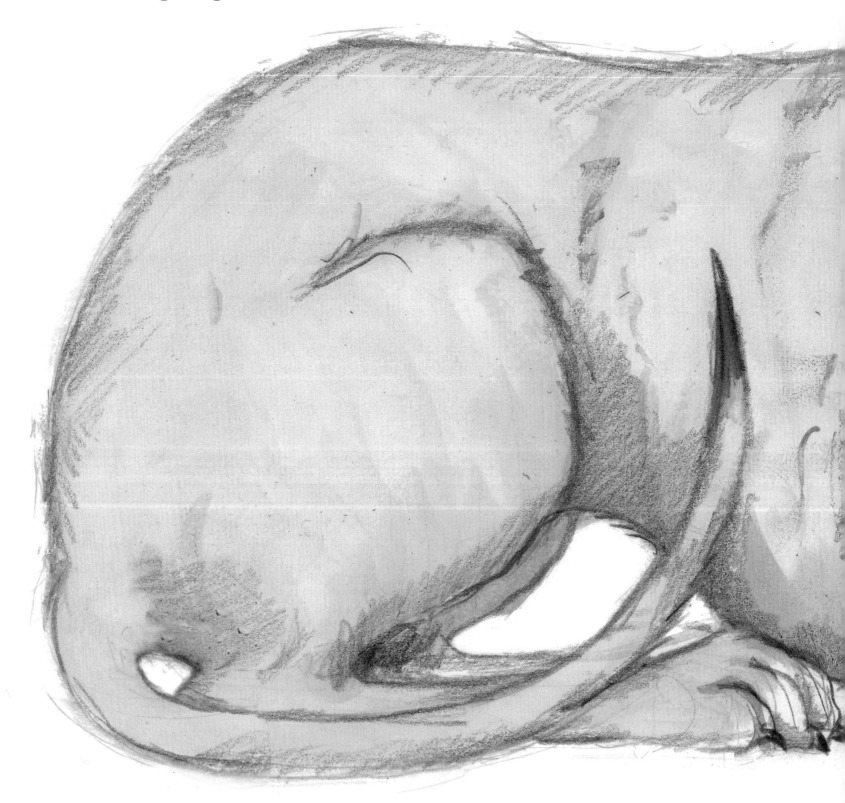

and small dogs.

I love stroppy dogs

and soppy dogs.

I love dogs that bark

and dogs that don't.

I love dogs that play

and dogs that won't.

I love hairy dogs

and bald dogs.

Stripy dogs

and spotty dogs.

I love slow dogs

and fast dogs.

Scruffy

and smart dogs.

I love dogs that are good

and dogs that are bad.

But the dog that I love best?
Let's see . . .

. . . is any dog

that won't chase me!

Great Dane          Dachshund          Shar Pei